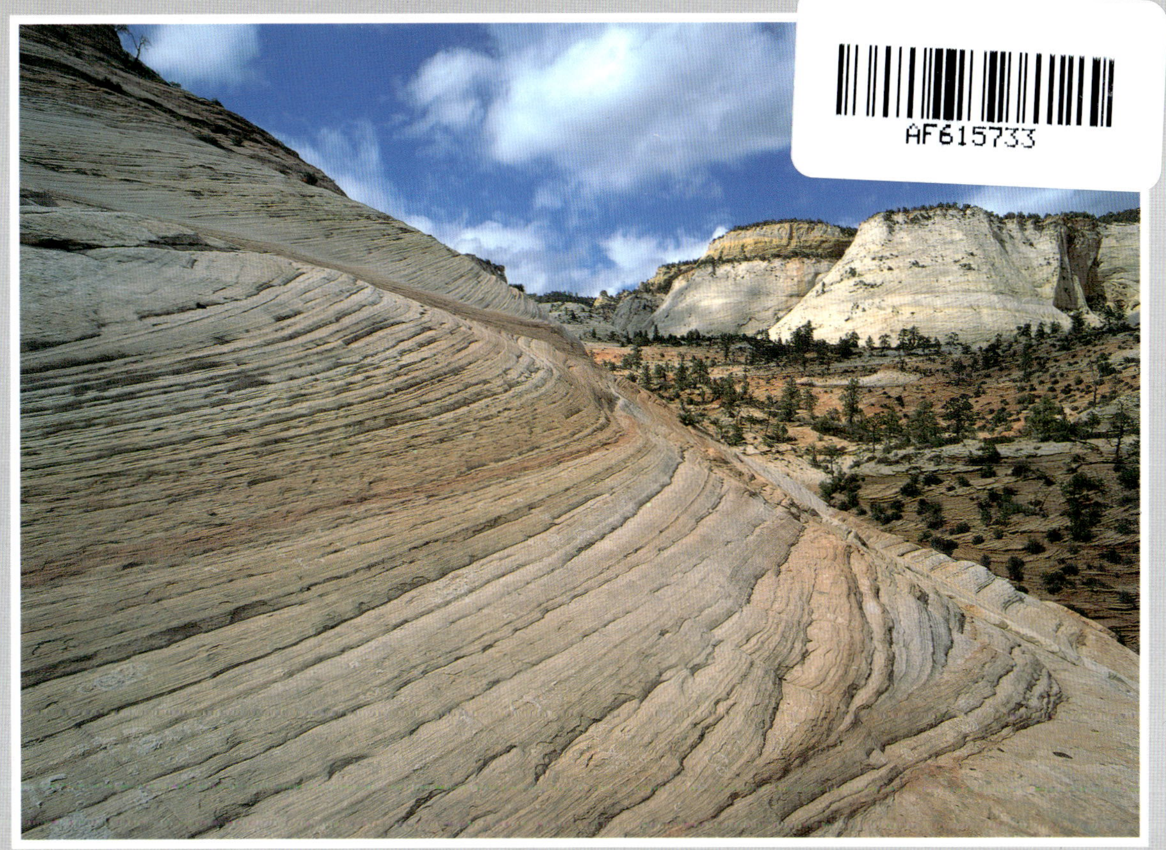

Cross-bedded Sandstone & White Cliffs. The high country of Zion is a wonderland of bizarre shapes and forms. The Navajo Sandstone which makes up this landscape was originally deposited as windblown sand dunes which stretched from central Wyoming to southwestern California. Seas which later covered this region provided the calcareous cementing materials which helped bond the sand together.

FIRST CLASS POSTAGE REQUIRED

From the WISH YOU WERE HERE® POSTCARD BOOK—ZION NATIONAL PARK

SIERRA PRESS: Visit us at www.nationalparksusa.com

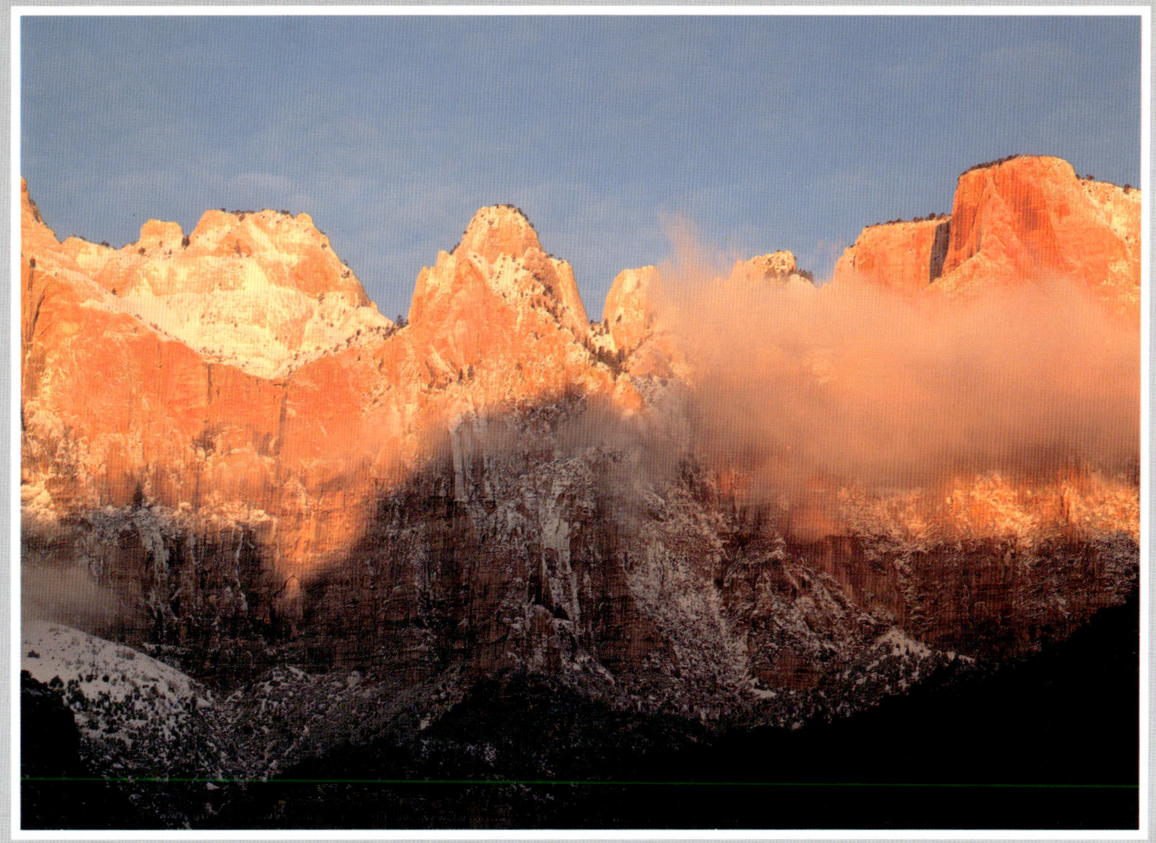

Towers of the Virgin, Winter Sunrise. Rising some 3000 feet above river level, The Towers of the Virgin form the headwall of the canyon of Oak Creek. The fine-grained sandstone which forms the wall has been stained by the iron-oxide rich Temple Cap formation which was deposited as water borne sediment and later eroded away. It was scenes like this that persuaded President Taft to set Zion Canyon aside as the 22nd addition to the National Park System on July 31, 1909.

From the WISH YOU WERE HERE® POSTCARD BOOK—ZION NATIONAL PARK

FIRST CLASS POSTAGE REQUIRED

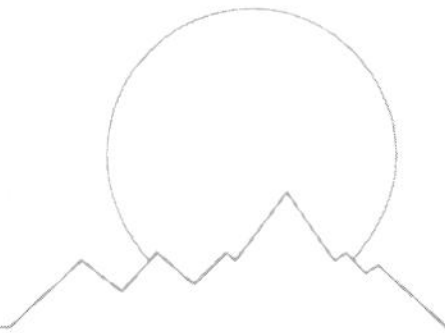

SIERRA PRESS: Visit us at www.nationalparksusa.com

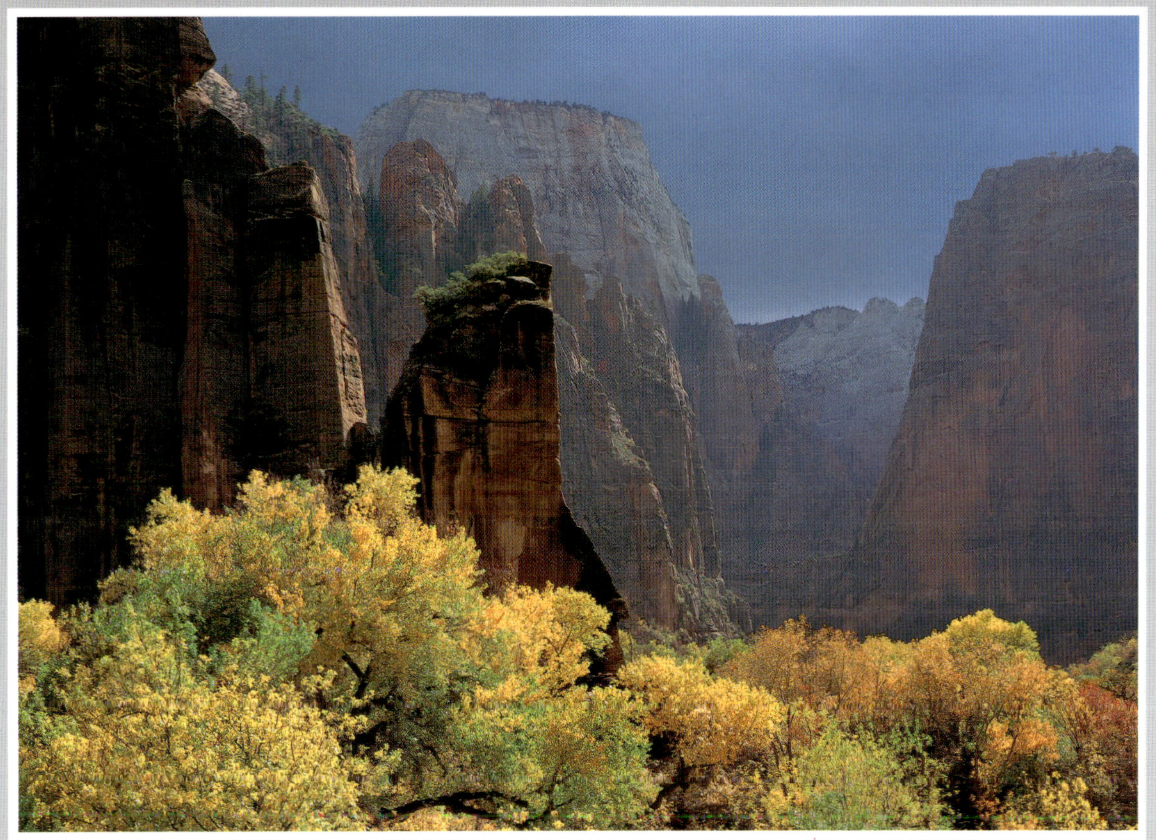

Cottonwoods & the Great White Throne. Originally named by Frederick Fisher, a visiting Methodist minister, the Great White Throne towers 2000 feet above the Virgin River at its feet. This singular monolith provides the visitor with perhaps the best view of the full depth of the Navajo Sandstone formation in this region. The sheer face of the 'Throne' is the result of joints in the stone. In this case we see one side of the joint, the other side having been undercut, leading to its falling away leaving the sheer wall we see today.

From the WISH YOU WERE HERE® POSTCARD BOOK – ZION NATIONAL PARK

FIRST CLASS POSTAGE REQUIRED

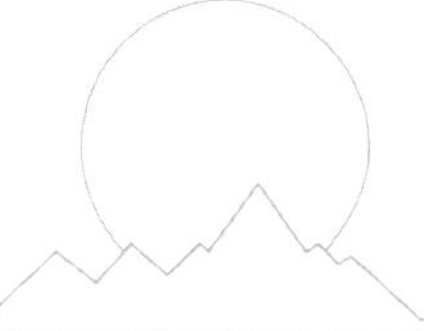

SIERRA PRESS: Visit us at www.nationalparksusa.com

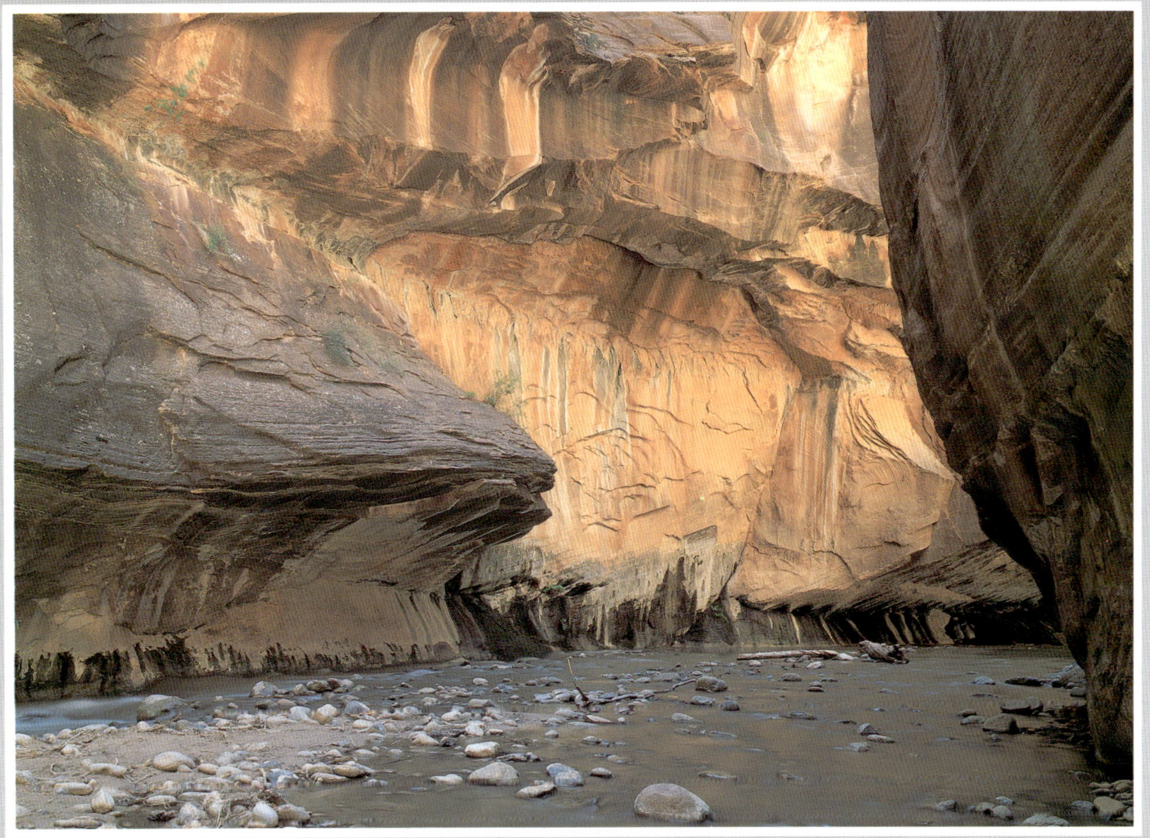

The Narrows of the Virgin River. Reached via a one mile trail which begins at roads end at the Temple of Sinawava, the Narrows is a spectacular gorge as little as 18 feet wide and as much as 2000 feet deep. This narrow slot is the result of the rapidly flowing waters of the North Fork of the Virgin River cutting into the soft, evenly grained Navajo Sandstone as it flows from the 9000 foot high Markagunt Plateau on its way to Lake Mead, some 200 miles distant.

FIRST
CLASS
POSTAGE
REQUIRED

From the WISH YOU WERE HERE® POSTCARD BOOK—ZION NATIONAL PARK

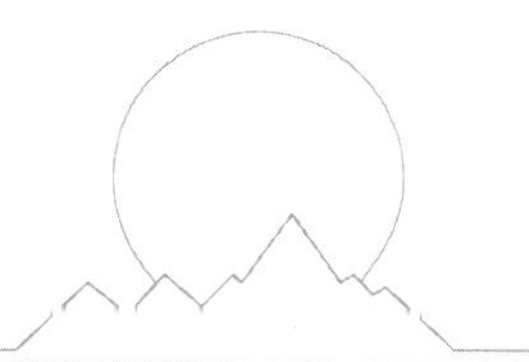

SIERRA PRESS: Visit us at www.nationalparksusa.com

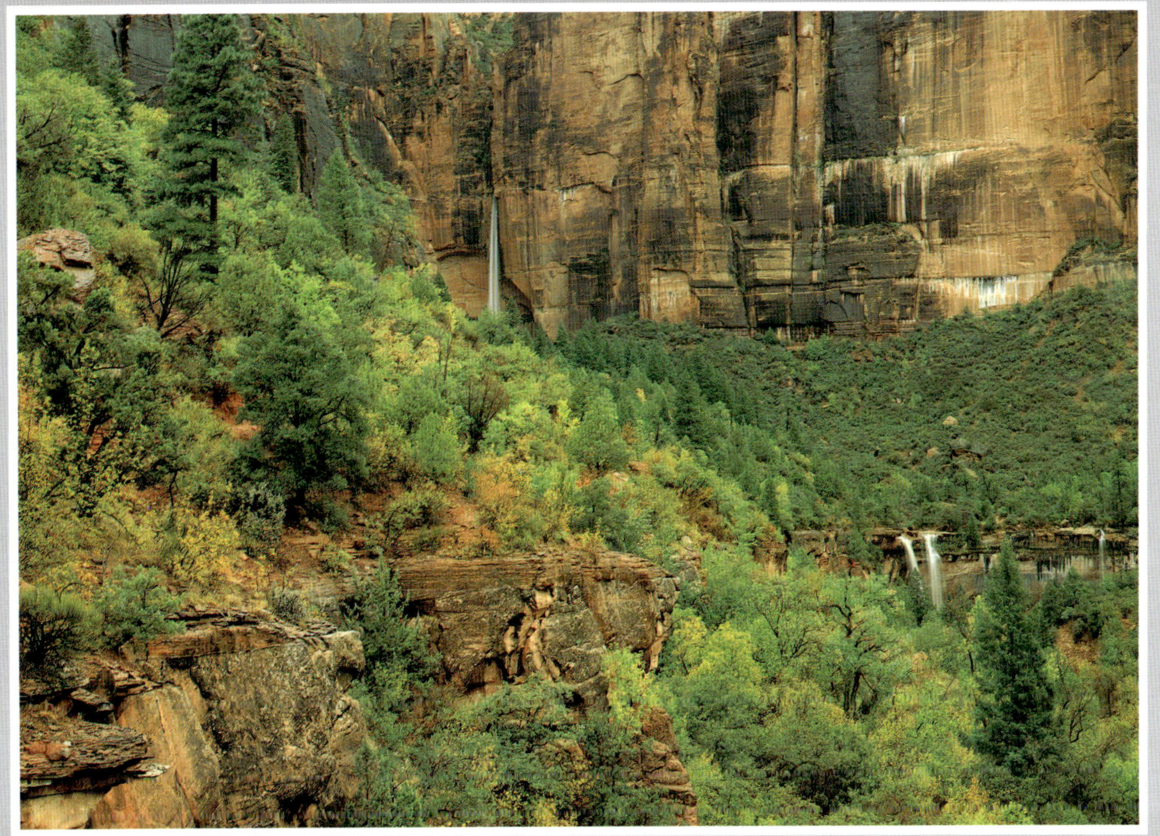

Heap Canyon & Waterfalls near Emerald Pools. Located across Zion Canyon from the lodge area, Heap Canyon is where the Emerald Pools are found. Here groves of oak, maple, ash, juniper, and fir lushly carpet the slopes as ephemeral falls from thundershowers and snowmelt as well as seeps from Zion's famous 'seepline' continue to gouge the algae-colored pools which give the area its name.

From the WISH YOU WERE HERE® POSTCARD BOOK—ZION NATIONAL PARK

FIRST CLASS POSTAGE REQUIRED

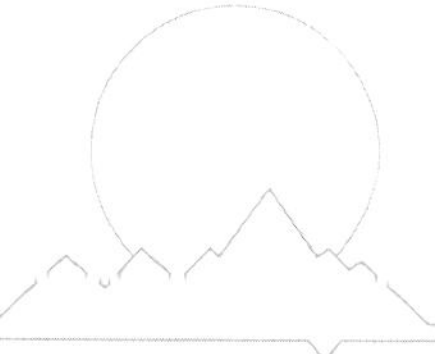

SIERRA PRESS: Visit us at www.nationalparksusa.com

PHOTO: © LARRY ULRICH

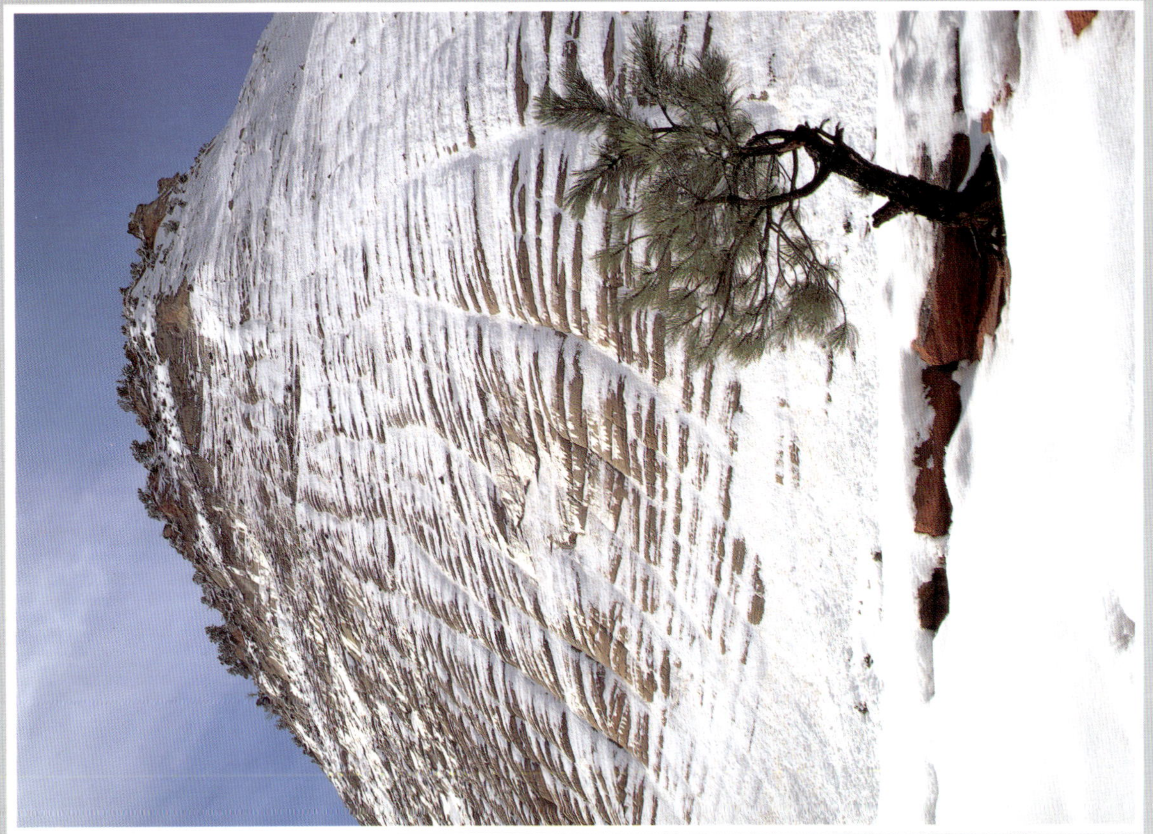

Checkerboard Mesa, Winter. The first named feature as the visitor enters the Park from the east, Checkerboard Mesa is a spectacular rounded sandstone form, seemingly overlaid with a 'fishnet'. This is the result of shallow vertical fractures, possibly caused by expansion and contraction, incised into the horizontal bedding layers of the Navajo Sandstone of which the mesa is formed. These vertical fractures are usually 6-13 inches deep and contribute to the gradual erosion of the mesa.

From the WISH YOU WERE HERE® POSTCARD BOOK—ZION NATIONAL PARK

FIRST
CLASS
POSTAGE
REQUIRED

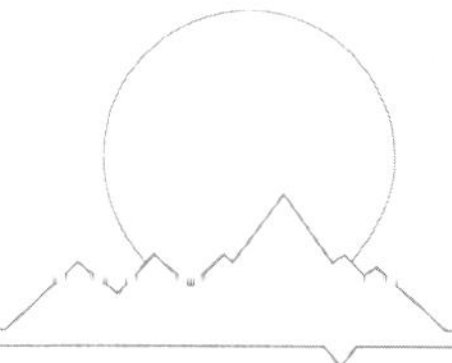

SIERRA PRESS: Visit us at www.nationalparksusa.com

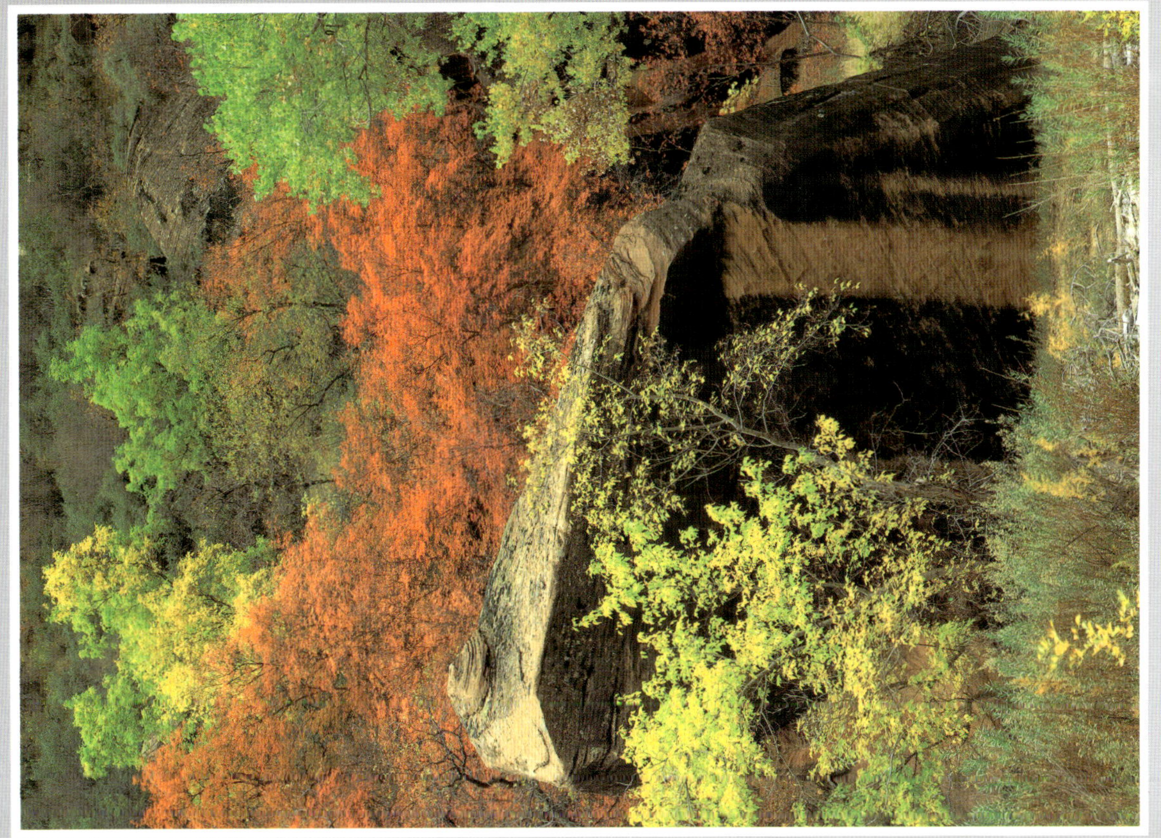

Autumn Color, Zion Canyon. The first-time visitor to Zion may be surprised by the diversity of plant life to be found in the Park. Variations in elevation, from 3666 to 8740 feet, as well as the availability of moisture contribute to a stunning mosaic of form, texture, and color. Seen here; big-toothed maple, willow, and fremont cottonwood create a kaleidoscope of fall color along the Virgin River.

From the WISH YOU WERE HERE® POSTCARD BOOK—ZION NATIONAL PARK

FIRST
CLASS
POSTAGE
REQUIRED

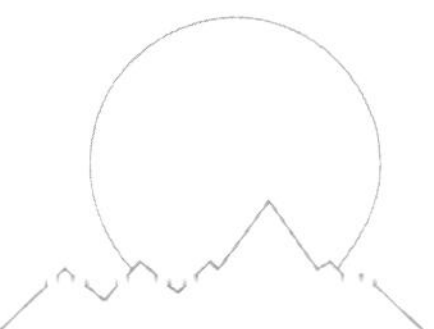

SIERRA PRESS: Visit us at www.nationalparksusa.com

PHOTO: © JIM WILSON

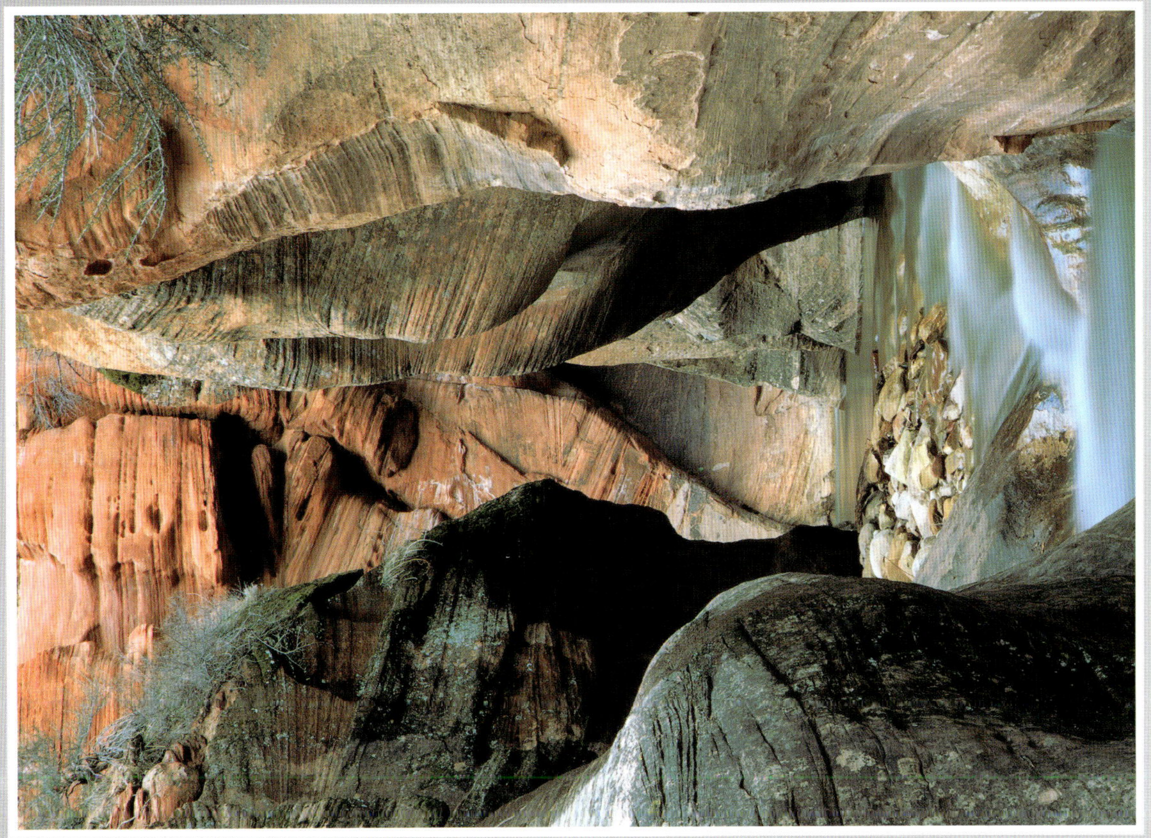

Echo Canyon. Seen from the East Rim Trail which begins at the Weeping Rock parking area, Echo Canyon is an astonishing slot which is still being carved by raging waters as they rush off Cable Mountain. Sublime scenes such as this await the adventurous hiker throughout the Zion landscape.

From the WISH YOU WERE HERE® POSTCARD BOOK—ZION NATIONAL PARK

FIRST CLASS POSTAGE REQUIRED

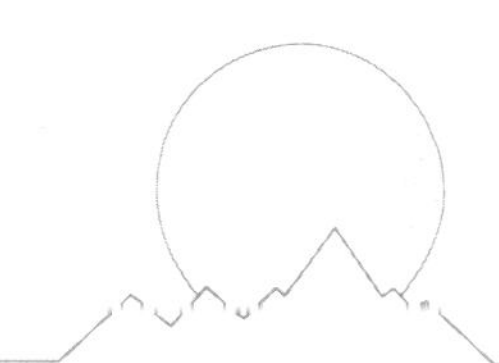

SIERRA PRESS: Visit us at www.nationalparksusa.com

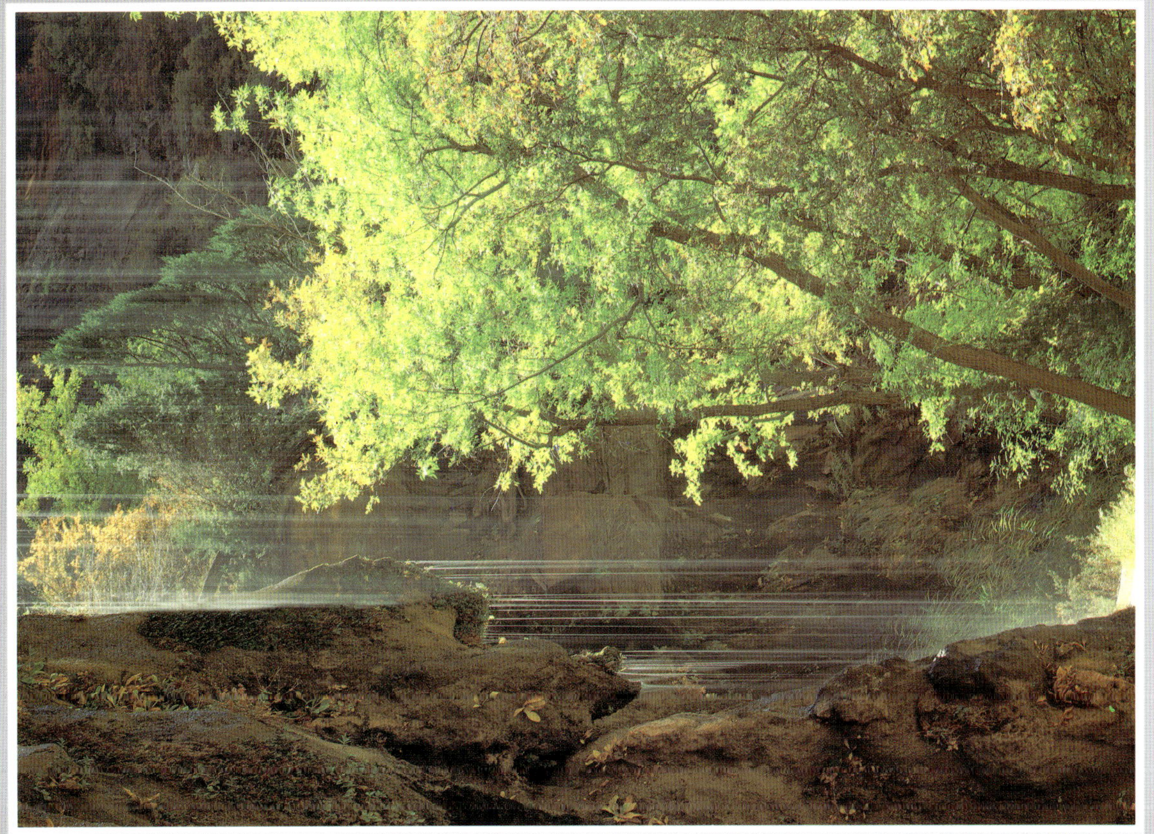

Weeping Rock. Springs and seeps play a major role in shaping the Zion Canyon we see today. The Navajo Sandstone, which is the 'top' of much of the Zion region, absorbs much of the rain and snow falling on it. This water percolates through the stone until it reaches the impervious Kayenta Formation which lies under the Navajo. At this point the water can only move horizontally, emerging from the walls of Zion Canyon and creating the 'springline'.

From the WISH YOU WERE HERE® POSTCARD BOOK—ZION NATIONAL PARK

FIRST CLASS POSTAGE REQUIRED

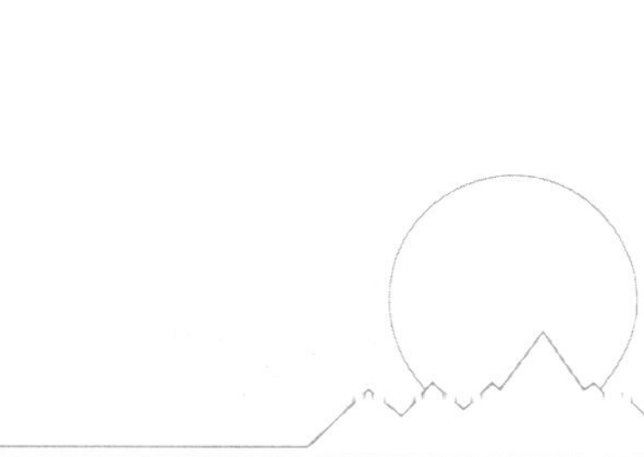

SIERRA PRESS: Visit us at www.nationalparksusa.com

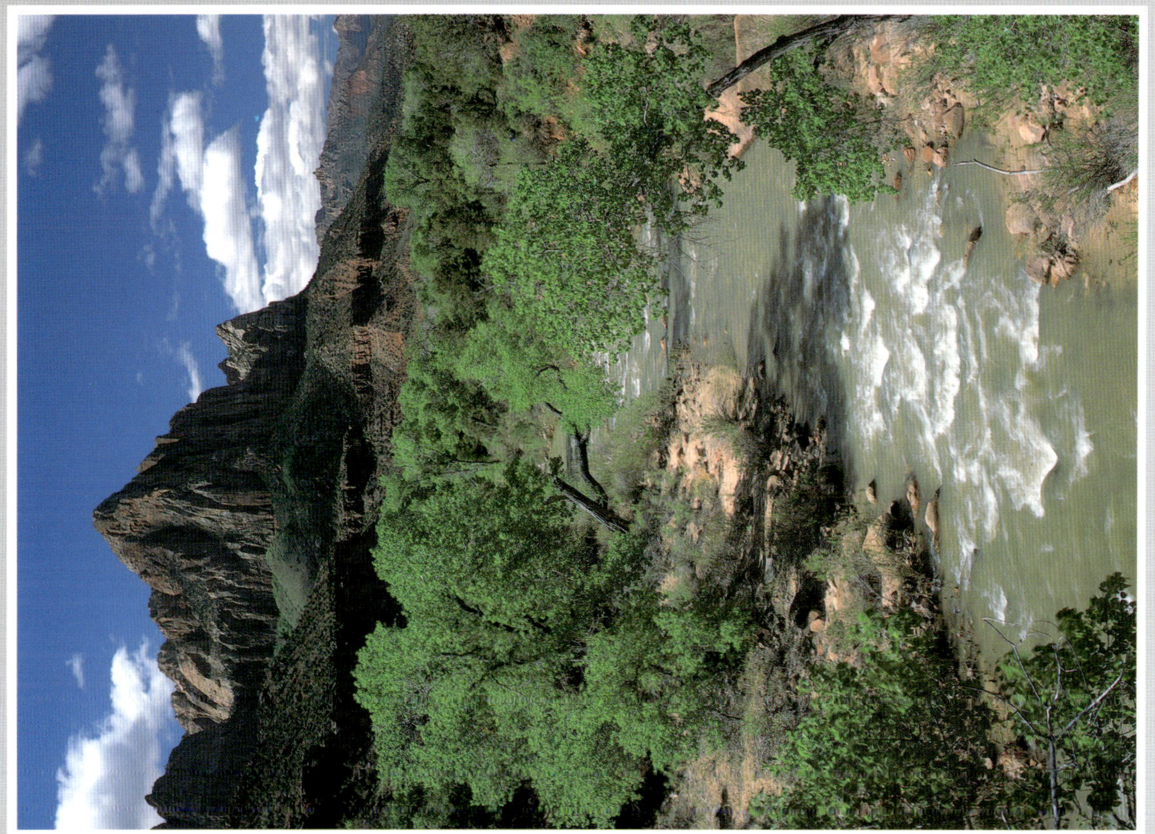

Virgin River & The Watchman. The seemingly placid waters of the North Fork of the Virgin River were almost entirely responsible for the erosion which created the Zion Canyon we see today. Transporting more than one million tons of sediments per year, the river is often referred to as being an endless, moving belt of sandpaper. Less than 200 miles in length, the Virgin River ultimately deposits its load of sediment into Lake Mead.

From the WISH YOU WERE HERE® POSTCARD BOOK—ZION NATIONAL PARK

FIRST
CLASS
POSTAGE
REQUIRED

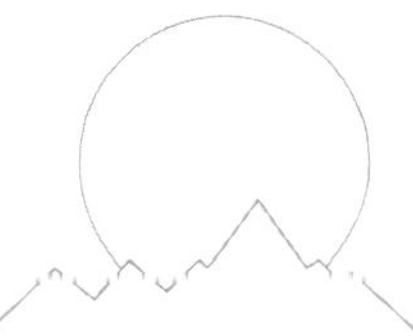

SIERRA PRESS: Visit us at www.nationalparksusa.com

PHOTO: © JEFF NICHOLAS

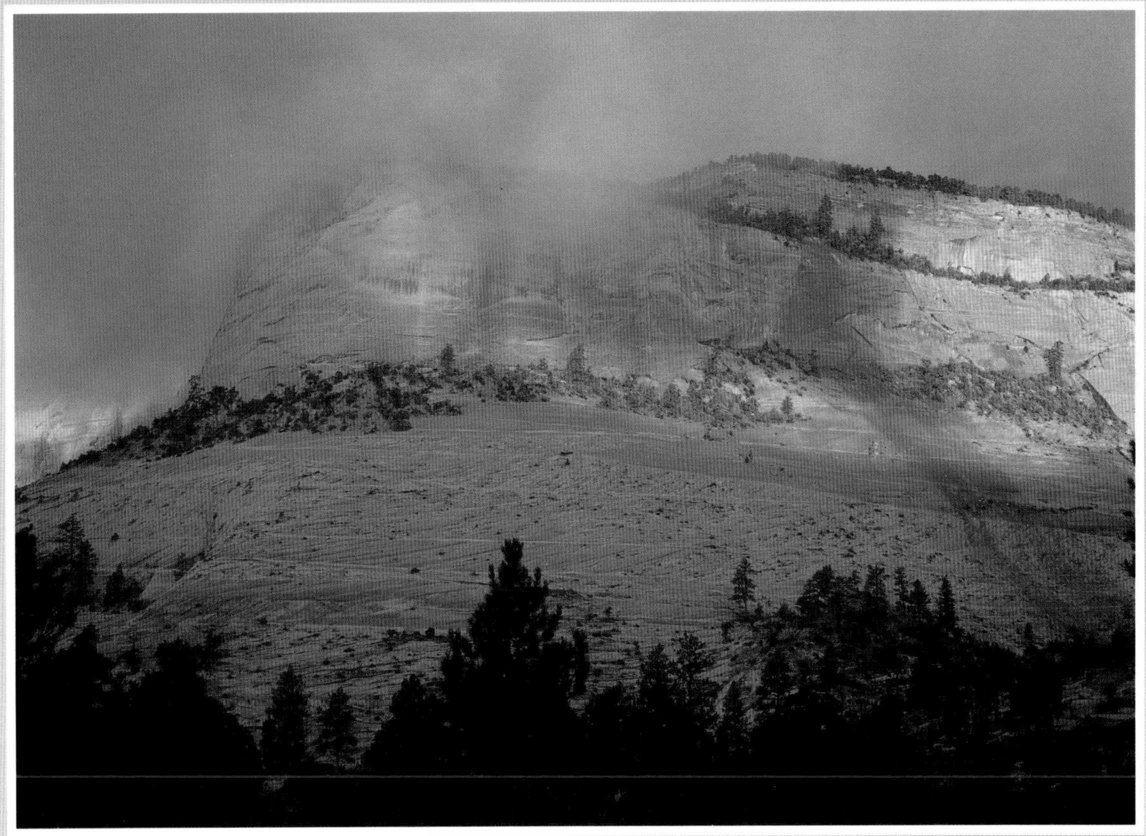

Clouds & Cliffs, East Rim. The stunning landscape of Zion, while dominated by forms carved into Navajo Sandstone, is actually made up of eight different formations, ranging in age from 220 to 53 million years. These layers tell the story of rivers, lakes, vast deserts, volcanoes, and gentle seas. Today's landscape is but a brief moment in geologic time and slow as it seems to us, great change is happening even today as earthquakes, gravity, erosion, and time continue to take their toll.

From the WISH YOU WERE HERE® POSTCARD BOOK—ZION NATIONAL PARK

FIRST
CLASS
POSTAGE
REQUIRED

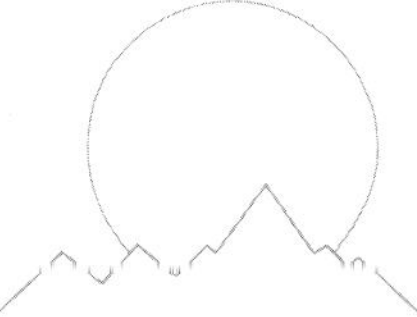

SIERRA PRESS: Visit us at www.nationalparksusa.com

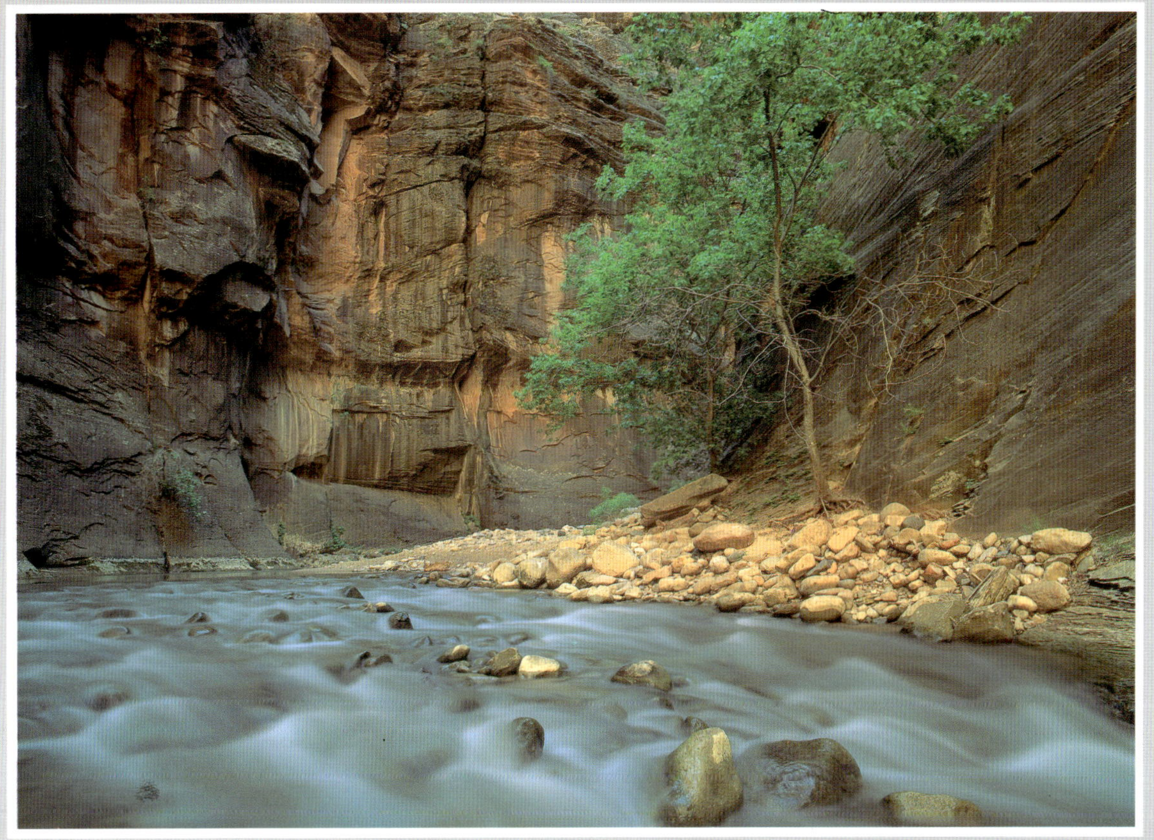

The Narrows of the Virgin River. Despite its calm appearance, the Virgin River drops up to 80 feet per mile here, ten times the gradient of the Colorado River as it flows through the Grand Canyon. This velocity, coupled with the sediments transported by the rapidly flowing waters have created a breathtaking gorge. Capt. George M. Wheeler, mapping this region in 1872 for the U.S. Government, proclaimed this "...the most wonderful defile it has been my fortune to behold."

From the WISH YOU WERE HERE® POSTCARD BOOK—ZION NATIONAL PARK

FIRST
CLASS
POSTAGE
REQUIRED

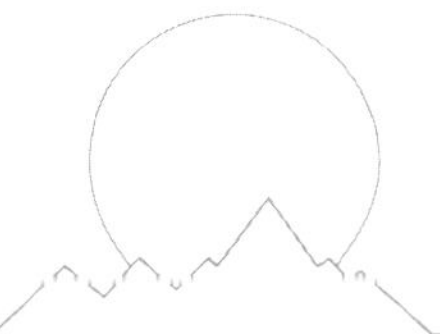

SIERRA PRESS: Visit us at www.nationalparksusa.com

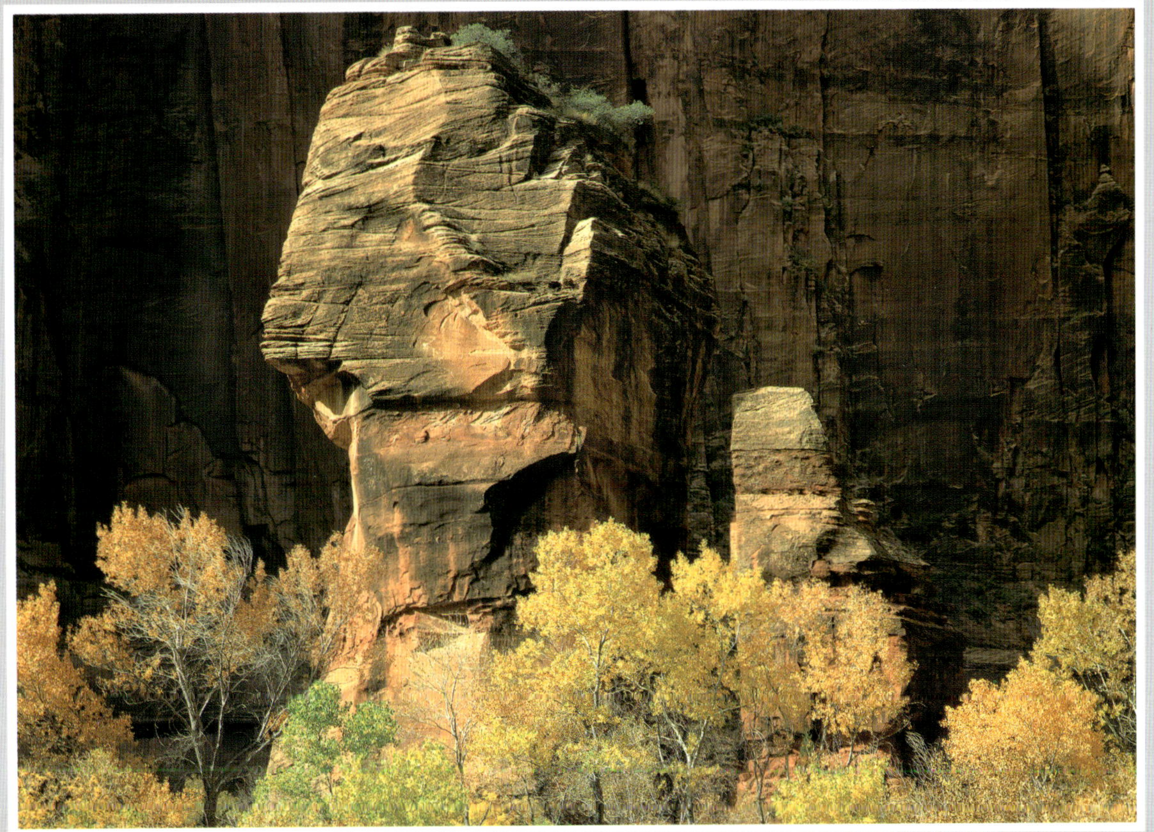

The Pulpit in the Temple of Sinawava. The 150 foot tall Pulpit is dwarfed by the 2000 foot walls of Navajo Sandstone which form the great 'Temple.' It is here that the Virgin River finally cuts through the bottom of the Navajo and strikes the softer Kayenta formation. This softer stone undercuts the Navajo, causing great blocks to shear off along joints in the rock, opening up the canyon. This provides both light and soil for the lush riparian habitat which borders the Virgin River as it flows from here down the length of Zion Canyon.

From the WISH YOU WERE HERE® POSTCARD BOOK—ZION NATIONAL PARK

FIRST CLASS POSTAGE REQUIRED

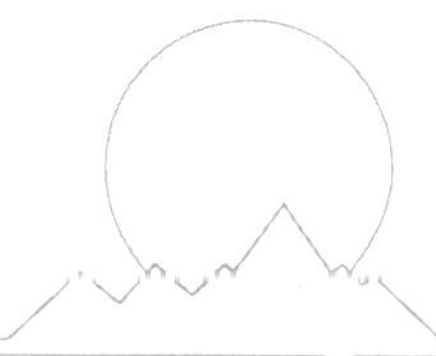

SIERRA PRESS: Visit us at www.nationalparksusa.com

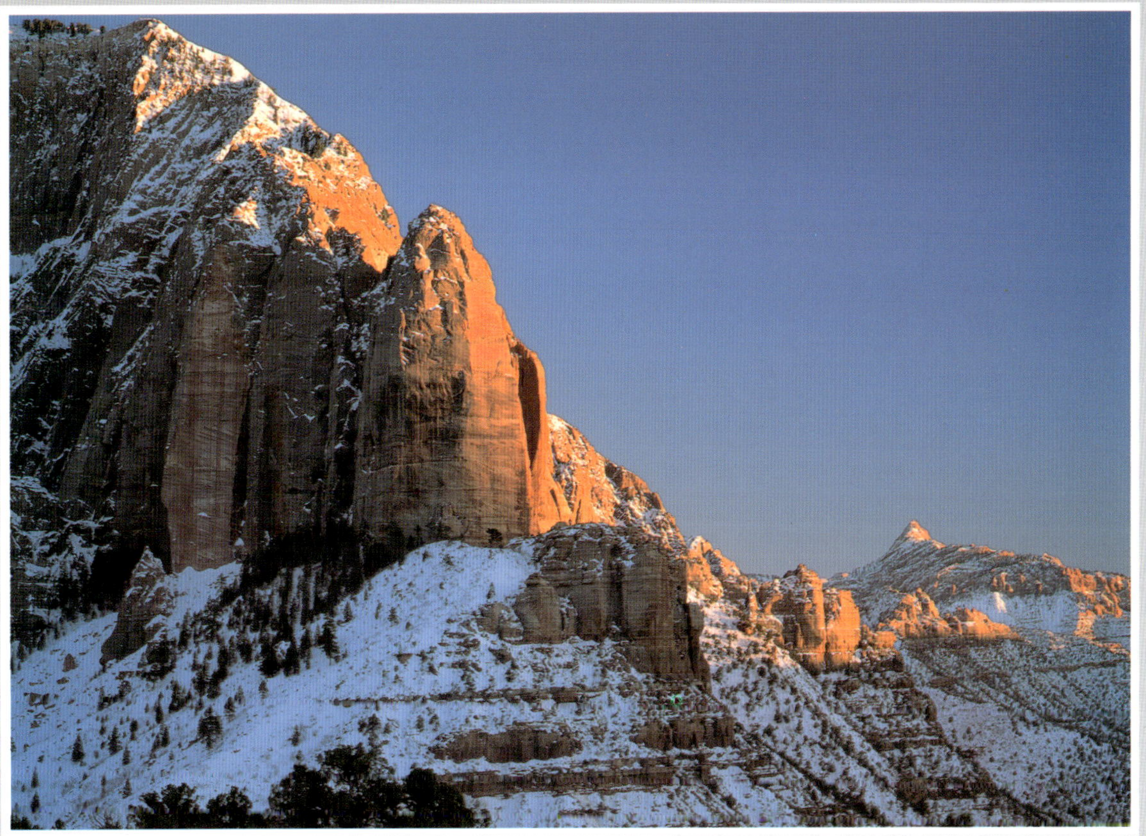

Kolob Terrace, Winter Sunset. The Kolob Terrace is the western edge of the Markagunt Plateau. Upthrust along the Hurricane Fault, the 'terrace' has been deeply etched into a series of 1600 foot deep 'finger' canyons. The world's largest arch, 310 foot Kolob Arch, is located here and can be reached via a 7 mile trail. Unlike Zion Canyon, whose upper walls are nearly white, here a rich salmon red hue colors the walls from top to bottom.

From the WISH YOU WERE HERE® POSTCARD BOOK—ZION NATIONAL PARK

FIRST CLASS POSTAGE REQUIRED

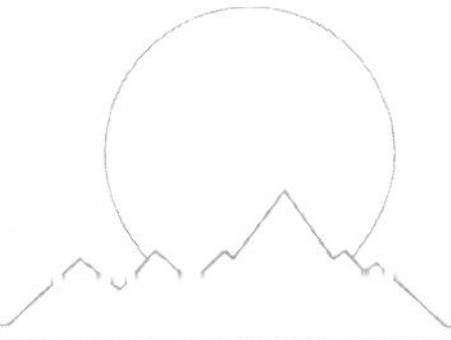

SIERRA PRESS: Visit us at www.nationalparksusa.com